REJOICE

Scripture, Prayers, and Poems for the More Abundant Life

Let the Earth REJOICE

Scripture, Prayers, and Poems
for the More Abundant Life

Joseph T. Nolan

ThomasMore®

Allen, Texas

Acknowledgments:

Scripture quotations are adapted from *The New Revised Standard Version* of the Bible, copyright 1989 by the Division of Christian Education of the National Council of the Churches of Christ in the USA. Used by permission. All rights reserved.

Cover design: Debbie Sheppard
Interior art & design: Barbara E. Mueller

Readers may contact the author at **nolanj@bc.edu.**

Send all inquiries to:

THOMAS MORE PUBLISHING
200 East Bethany Drive
Allen, Texas 75002-3804

Telephone: 877-275-4725 / 972-390-6300

Fax: 800-688-8356 / 972-390-6560

Customer Service e-mail: **cservice@rcl-enterprises.com**

Web site: **www.ThomasMore.com**

Printed in the United States of America

Library of Congress Catalog Number 00133319

ISBN 0-88347-464-6

1 2 3 4 5   04 03 02 01 00

Contents

Dedication

To Joseph O'Connell Swindal,
Thomas Joseph Cavanaugh Choy,
Nolan Christopher Vyhnal and their families,
with love

Introduction

For many years I have rejoiced in a calling that allows one to speak of life, love, and death, and relate them all to the mystery of God. For Christians all this begins with the One who is God's gift to us, Jesus Christ, and is helped by the gift both Father and Son promised, the Holy Spirit. In Christian worship we meet to break bread, as Jesus once did with sinners (and still does). We read the texts from his own people (the Hebrew scriptures) and from those faith communities who gave us the gospels. And there are letters from the incredible Paul, letters that pour out doctrines, snatches of hymns, prayers, and early sermons. Every Sunday we hear prophets and poets, apostles and evangelists. All this, of course, is the Bible. Some parts are wonderfully easy to understand. Others are not; we need the help of learned and prayerful people.

And of poets. It is no false humility to disclaim being a great poet—just read the great ones—but I wish to tell the Good News with imagination, and a sense of playfulness, and metaphors that help communication. Or really, communion—with truth, delight, goodness. These offerings seek to allow God's Word entrance to the heart and evoke a response not only in prayer but in life. Some of them are rather pointed, like the prophet Nathan saying, "You are the man." Or the woman. It is you whom God is addressing. Others have a wry humor, and there is humor in the gospel accounts. Think of Peter sinking below the surface of the water, or the woman at the well who just couldn't get the point, or the dismayed wine sellers of Cana, or the herdsmen of the swine who see their flock go over the cliff so this rabbi, known as Jesus, could make his point.

Some have come out of trial, or pain, such as the final one, "A Woman Clothed with the Sun." I wanted to appropriate that apocalyptic passage and anticipate the day when we join the company of the blessed, when each of us hopes to be clothed with the sun. It was written for those autumn years when God completes the work begun in each of us. Our time is so brief in terms of history, so glorious in the light of eternity, and so wonderful that it happened at all.

My favorite of these poems is "God of Harmony, Let Me Dance". I really do think that we are destined for joy and should anticipate it now.

A note on the opening poem, "Prayer for the Planet." I used this to conclude an address at Norfolk, Virginia; it was a convocation of chaplains, theologians, and top naval brass to discuss the ethical issues of war, especially with our world-destroying weapons. Flying into Norfolk you pass over what looks like a steel forest. It is the Atlantic fleet, at anchor, ready. It is massed power, with highly trained and committed people. We have another kind of power, and Christ wishes us to use it to bring about the reign of God.

Rev. Joseph T. Nolan
Boston College

Reflections

The scriptures are to meditate as well as to preach; these reflections offer another way to put the text in context. John's gospel ends with these words:

> *But there are also many other things that Jesus did; if every one of them were written down, I suppose that the world itself could not contain the books that would be written (John 21:25).*

Think of all the books and sermons on what he did say and do, offered with the hope that they are guided by the Holy Spirit. There is another "ending" to John's gospel (John 20:30-31) which is the reassurance that only grace can give:

> *Now Jesus did many other signs in the presence of his disciples, which are not written in this book. But these are written so that you may come to believe that Jesus is the Messiah, the Son of God, and that through believing you may have life in his name.*

Prayer for the Planet

Then God said, "Let us make humankind in our image, according to our likeness; and let them have dominion over the fish of the sea, and over the birds of the air, and over the cattle, and over all the wild animals of the earth, and over every creeping thing that creeps upon the earth."

So God created humankind in his image, in the image of God he created them; male and female he created them.

God blessed them, and God said to them, "Be fruitful and multiply, and fill the earth and subdue it; and have dominion over the fish of the sea and over the birds of the air and over every living thing that moves upon the earth." God said, "See, I have given you every plant yielding seed that is upon the face of all the earth, and every tree with seed in its fruit; you shall have them for food. And to every beast of the earth, and to every bird of the air, and to everything that creeps on the earth, everything that has the breath of life, I have given every green plant for food." And it was so. God saw everything that he had made, and indeed, it was very good . . .

Genesis 1:26-31

Lord, as far as we know,
this is your favorite planet.
Forgive some of the things
    we have done to it:
to the air, the water, the earth.
We have reason to think
that we curious bipeds
are your special creation.
We have found no one else
on the moon, Mars, or Jupiter
who makes music, love and wine.
Forgive what we do to each other.
We forget that you like variety
and made us in five colors,
singing different songs.
Lord, we live on that blue marble
you spun off when you played creation.
It is a lovely place.
Help us to keep it
in one peace.

Divinity

If we really knew the glory
of Jesus as divine
the stars would tremble
and the sun refuse to shine.
Humanity reveals him
and also conceals him.

Let There Be Light

And God said, "Let there be lights in the dome of
the sky to separate the day from the night; and let
them be for signs and for seasons and for days and
years, and let them be lights in the dome of the sky
to give light upon the earth." And it was so. God
made the two great lights—the greater light to rule
the day and the lesser light to rule the night—and
the stars. God set them in the dome of the sky to
give light upon the earth, to rule over the day and
over the night, and to separate the light from the
darkness. And God saw that it was good. And there
was evening and there was morning, the fourth day.
Genesis 1:14-19

All creation's needlepoint.
Done fine, and finer.
Nothing swabbed, or daubed. It is not lobbed
with mops of paint from brimming buckets.
The distant eye deceives, sees only
blue patches, walls of water, azure skies.
Come nearer. The heart has eyes.
The formless mist turns into pendants,
each its cosmos.
The leaf is teeming, and the stony mass
an airy planet called molecular
where bits and pieces, crafted in the fire,
dance to electronic measures.
Mark how they bow and yield,
go round in merry orbits, do all but
make the music of the spheres that
perhaps is sung, if we had ears to hear.

What Keeps Us Going?

*The LORD created me at the beginning of his work, the
first of his acts of long ago. Ages ago I was set up, at
the first, before the beginning of the earth. When there
were no depths I was brought forth, when there were
no springs abounding with water. Before the mountains
had been shaped, before the hills, I was brought
forth—when he had not yet made earth and fields, or
the world's first bits of soil. When he established the
heavens, I was there, when he drew a circle on the face
of the deep, when he made firm the skies above, when
he established the fountains of the deep, when he
assigned to the sea its limit, so that the waters might
not transgress his command, when he marked out the
fountains of the earth, then I was beside him, like a
master worker; and I was daily his delight, rejoicing
before him always, rejoicing in his inhabited world
and delighting in the human race.*

Proverbs 8:22-31

*Where can I go from your spirit? Or where can I flee
from your presence? If I ascend to heaven, you are
there; if I make my bed in Sheol, you are there. If I
take the wings of the morning and settle at the farthest
limits of the sea, even there your hand shall lead me,
and your right hand shall hold me fast.*

Psalm 139:7-10

A new heart I will give you, and a new spirit I will put within you; and I will remove from your body the heart of stone and give you a heart of flesh. I will put my spirit within you, and make you follow my statutes and be careful to observe my ordinances.

Ezekiel 36:26-27

What is it, Lord, that makes some people
so good with black marks upon a page?
They turn all those wriggles into meaning,
blots and circles into music.
Who makes a music maker—and a poet?
All that scratched-out heap of words
suddenly a cut diamond, budded rose.

Who put this mind in matter?
The mystery starts early.
No one seems to teach us
how to laugh, draw pictures,
or tumble into language.
How much, . . . how much is gift?

The earth spins so carefully.
You set this gyroscope,
gave it a sun, and sprinkled our night
      with stars.
Day returns, and spring.
Who makes hope return,
and love, like long-damped fires, start again?

Who makes us lovers, shapers, makers,
clowns and carpenters and bakers,
more than numbers, height, and weight?
What keeps us going,
raises us so often from the dead?
Why were games we played so much fun,
and why did we forget so soon
the secret children never have to learn
of how to play, to make time nothing?

A voice speaks, not on mountains and
            in thunder
but suddenly it is Sinai.
"I will put my spirit in you, and you will live."

Let Me Never Be Ashamed
to Bear Witness

Paul, an apostle of Christ Jesus by the will of God,
for the sake of the promise of life that is in Christ
Jesus, To Timothy, my beloved child: Grace, mercy,
and peace from God the Father and Christ Jesus our
Lord . . . rekindle the gift of God that is within you
through the laying on of my hands; for God did not
give us a spirit of cowardice, but rather a spirit of
power and of love and of self-discipline.

2 Timothy 1:1-2, 6-7

My loving God, I pray to you,
mindful of your gifts to me
when the hands of your anointed
were laid upon me
in those holy sacraments
that made me a temple of the Spirit
and my soul like a candle
received the light of faith.

Let me never be ashamed to bear witness
nor be fearful of the cross.
Let me remember that the Spirit given to me
is no cowardly spirit
but one that comes in power and grace
to make me a strong and loving person.

I thank you for all that I have learned
from faithful and loving teachers
about Jesus, Lord and Savior,

and I ask your help to guard
the rich deposit of faith
that has been passed on to me
by all the generations who have heard
the Gospel and sought to follow Christ.

O Lord, I have one more prayer:
You who has given me your good Spirit,
with whom all things are possible,
make me strong, loving, and wise.

Is That Me, Lord?

*Alas for those who are at ease in Zion, and for those
who feel secure on Mount Samaria, the notables of the
first of the nations, to whom the house of Israel
resorts! . . . Alas for those who lie on beds of ivory,
and lounge on their couches, and eat lambs from the
flock, and calves from the stall; who sing idle songs to
the sound of the harp, and like David improvise on
instruments of music; who drink wine from bowls, and
anoint themselves with the finest oils, but are not
grieved over the ruin of Joseph! Therefore they shall
now be the first to go into exile, and the revelry of the
loungers shall pass away.*

Amos 6:1, 4-7

I've read this passage from Amos
and took thought upon it, and decided
whomever he's talking about,
it's not me!

The prophet scorns those who "lie upon beds
    of ivory."
I've used a waterbed,
and a mahogany bedstead,
but I haven't been on a bed of ivory in
    my life.

Then he gets riled about people
"stretched comfortably on their couches."
That's me! But what's the harm?
And what's wrong with

"eating spring lamb and fine veal"?
There's more gustatory talk;
he says the crowds around him
"drink wine from bowls
and anoint themselves with their best oils."

Is that me?
We do have some pretty good
    cocktail parties,
some real bashes.
I guess you could say the women (the
    men, too)
"anoint themselves with the best oils."
We don't exactly drink from bowls—
those were pagans, weren't they—
but we drink. We drink a lot.
We wreck our cars with our drinking.
Sometimes we wreck our lives.
"They drink from bowls," he said.
I'm not so sure I can say, not me!
But not that "wanton revelry" stuff.
Oh, we entertain, we keep a full bar.
We have three cars,
we can't wear
all the clothes we keep on buying.
We even throw out a lot of food
and the kids spend like crazy
on their stereos and their cars.
But "wanton revelry"? Not us.

One thing that bothers me;
it's the way Amos starts off.
"Woe to you complacent!"
What does that mean? I'm not sure,
except—it can't be me.

We Have Not Seen . . .
and We Believe

We believe in God whom we do not see
because of Jesus who was seen
and people who live by his Spirit.

We believe in God whom we do not see
because of truth and beauty,
love, goodness, and integrity,
which make the divine a part of human life.

We believe in a heaven we have not seen
because love is stronger than death
and all our hopes
cannot find fulfillment in this life.

We believe in the Spirit we cannot see
because we see the Creator Spirit
at work in our lives
and hear the Spirit's voice in our silence.

We believe in the earth and its people
in spite of the evil we see
because we have shared their goodness.

We believe in the church we see
with its saints and sinners
because it has given us the Word
and gathered us in the breaking of the bread.

We believe in a providence we do not
always see
because God made us,
and here we are,
with ten billion years behind us.

We believe in the resurrection
in spite of the death we see
because we have been raised up many times,
and passed from death to life.

We believe in God whom we do not see
because of the One who said,
"He who sees me sees the Father."

We have seen him in our humanity,
in his risen body,
and we believe.

Incarnation

Hide divinity in a child.
Hide it so well
that many never listen
to what angels sing and prophets tell,
never walk where shepherds trod,
never see the face of God.

Savior

Door that opens wide,
gate of a pasture green inside,
water washing sins away,
sun that ushers in the day.

I'm Just . . . Me!

See, I am sending my messenger to prepare the way before me.

Malachi 3:1

Do not ask who the messenger is.
It is you.

You're thinking,
"I'm neither angel nor evangel.
I'm just a woman. Or a man."
Or, as the prophet Jeremiah once said
(also copping out),
"I'm just a child, you can't mean me."

But you're human.
And that's what God became.
That's the great secret of his hiding place,
that we keep so well
even from ourselves.

It's time to be a messenger
and let the world in on the secret.
Let the Word again take flesh.

God is love. Be loving.
God is passionate. Be forgiving.
God is just. Act with integrity.
God is one. Don't tear things apart.

God is joy. Be joyful.
God is creator. Be creative.
God is life. Choose life.
God is spirit. Be alive.

Fulfillment

I have said these things to you so that my joy may be in you, and that your joy may be complete.

John 15:11

Our time is so brief in terms of history,
so glorious in the light of eternity,
and so wonderful that it happened at all.

You Are All Things to Me

*As the Father has loved me, so I have loved you; abide
in my love. I have said these things to you so that my
joy may be in you, and that your joy may be complete.*

John 15:9-11

O God of all gods, parent beloved,
who desired me, made me,
O thou lover, dancer, singer within my soul,
from this day forward
I wish to undertake nothing
without first being gladdened
     by the thought of thee.

Thou art all things to me,
joy of my joy,
heart of my loving.
Help me by your Spirit
to live this day your life.

We Are the Work of Your Hands

Would that you might meet us doing right, that we were mindful of you in our ways! Behold, you are angry, and we are sinful; all of us have become like unclean men, all our good deeds are like polluted rags; we have all withered like leaves, and our guilt carries us away like the wind. There is none who calls upon your name, who rouses himself to cling to you; For you have hidden your face from us and have delivered us up to our guilt. Yet, O LORD, you are our father; we are the clay and you the potter: we are all the work of your hands. Be not so very angry, LORD, keep not our guilt forever in mind; look upon us, who are all your people.

Isaiah 64:4-8

God, is there a mistake somewhere?
What have you made us?

Leaves that wither,
blown by the mindless wind,
marked for the burning.

Broken vessels,
empty of good wine,
no longer lifted
to the lips of the living.

Shards that bury
in the debris of time.

Clay in the potter's hands.
The wheel turns,
the potter molds tomorrow.
The tree of Christ,
breaking the skies,
alive in the wind.

Invocation

O Trinity of gentle power,
hear us in this hour
of worship that we give to thee.
Set us free from human fears
and fill our years
with feelings of eternity.
Thou sun before whom fades the night,
give us thy light!
Give us thy light!

Incarnation

And God said to the blind,
"There are three persons
you do not see.
Yourself.
Your neighbor.
And me.
I want you to look at someone
and see all three."

The Whole Earth's a Waiting Room

Beware, keep alert; for you do not know when the time will come. It is like a man going on a journey, when he leaves home and puts his slaves in charge, each with his work, and commands the doorkeeper to be on the watch. Therefore, keep awake—for you do not know when the master of the house will come, in the evening, or at midnight, or at cockcrow, or at dawn, or else he may find you asleep when he comes suddenly. And what I say to you I say to all: Keep awake.

Mark 13:33-37

We wait—all day long,
for planes and buses,
for dates and appointments,
for five o'clock and Friday.

Some of us wait for a Second Coming.
For God in a whirlwind.
Paratrooper Christ.

All around us people are waiting:
a child, for attention;
a spouse, for conversation;
a parent, for a letter or call.

The prisoner waits for freedom;
and the exile, to come home.
The hungry, for food;
and the lonely, for a friend.

The whole earth's a waiting room!
"The Savior will see you now"
is what we expect to hear at the end.

Maybe we should raise our expectations.
The Savior might see us now
if we know how to find him.
Could it be that Jesus, too, is waiting
for us to know that he is around?

Advent

If the Dow is plunging
and inflation lunging,
war threatening
and earthquakes rumbling,
be of good cheer,
the end is not here.
And the Lord is near!

Christmas

Yes, Virginia, there is a Jesus
and Christmas is his story.
The prophets foretold him,
the heavens could not hold him,
and we shall see his glory.

We Need to Hear the Story

In the sixth month the angel Gabriel was sent by God to a town in Galilee called Nazareth, to a virgin engaged to a man whose name was Joseph, of the house of David. The virgin's name was Mary. And he came to her and said, "Greetings, favored one! The Lord is with you." But she was much perplexed by his words and pondered what sort of greeting this might be. The angel said to her, "Do not be afraid, Mary, for you have found favor with God. And now, you will conceive in your womb and bear a son, and you will name him Jesus. He will be great, and will be called the Son of the Most High, and the Lord God will give to him the throne of his ancestor David. He will reign over the house of Jacob forever, and of his kingdom there will be no end." Mary said to the angel, "How can this be, since I am a virgin?" The angel said to her, "The Holy Spirit will come upon you, and the power of the Most High will overshadow you; therefore the child to be born will be holy; he will be called Son of God. And now, your relative Elizabeth in her old age has also conceived a son; and this is the sixth month for her who was said to be barren. For nothing will be impossible with God." Then Mary said, "Here am I, the servant of the Lord; let it be with me according to your word." Then the angel departed from her.

Luke 1:26-38

Come, Luke and Matthew, tell us once
again—
it doesn't wear for telling—the story of
    our kinsman
born so long ago, this night called holy.
Had they money for the journey, did they plan
to stop where caravans put in, and found
    no room,
or did they ask for shelter in the cave
where friendly beasts would not intrude
or babble on about a census,
where one could find a quiet space
for a woman big with child, whose time
    had come?

Tell us how the poor came first to see him
with royalty and wealth to follow after
(the world turned upside down so soon).
A shepherd-king grants audience to
    eager subjects!
Then shift from innocence, to where
    another ruler
calls learned counselors at his murderous court.
Mark how they read out the word they do
    not heed:
"Bethlehem of Juda, thou are not so small!"
while those more wise
hear in silence and go on to seek the child.

We need to hear the story
for there's no great rush to find him now,
no tired feet or burning hearts.
Once more he is the seeker
and now we keep the inn, quite able
to refuse him entrance, to report no room.

How often have we re-made that resting place
in wood and marble, paint and stone,
and piled the clean straw around a
    shining infant,
setting his parents in adoring pose.
A cradle's easier to rearrange
than the furniture of the heart.
Where do you sleep tonight, eternal pilgrim?

God of Harmony, Let Me Dance

We say of Christmas, " 'Tis the season to
    be merry."
For everything there is a time.
We cannot laugh all the time,
but we have forgotten that we are made
in the image of a God who is joy as well
    as love.

Lord, help me to have fun.
I'm asking you because
a God who invented butterflies and ducks
must know something about it.
Remind me to have a good time.
Let me spend money as well as save it,
and spend it on someone besides myself.
I would feast as well as fast,
change water into wine,
and each day rediscover
that you have crammed the earth
    with surprises.

Let me use my body delightfully.
You built it, with its fine tuning
and that flexible thumb!
I am marvelously made.
You muscled my bones and thatched
    my head
and waited two million years for your manchild
to stand tall in the wind.

God of joy, give me your good Spirit!
God of harmony, let me dance

to the rhythms of your world!
I think you have a good time with
    your creation.
You pour out the oceans from your cup
and roll them like a bowling ball into
    the shore.
You beat out the sun, while the stars
fell in showers from your hammer.
You put the hummingbird together
and tossed an eagle into the air.
When the planets are dull you watch
    the children
swing to the top of the trees.

Lord of the rainbow and the redwood,
I can't take in
all five rings of your circus.
Give me more than five senses
and one time around.
Lord, I want to enjoy your life.

.

Christmas

Angels seek for shepherds
and kings look for a stable.
O things were really upside down
in Bethlehem town!
He began that very night
to set the world aright.

To shepherds and their sheep
and oxen in a stall,
to a carpenter and his wife,
to folk both great and small,
he comes—the babe of Bethlehem
whose love will save us all.

Shepherds Run and Wise Men Ponder

Mother of the One
who makes us one,
Virgin Mother
who received the word
first in silence,
then in flesh.

You gave him birth, the child
whose hands could play with stars
and toss the planets for his ball,
hands held out to gather in
the brother-sisterhood of earth.

Shepherds run and wise men ponder,
stars become a lantern
at the house of bread
where David's son holds court!

Son of Mary,
falling on us like the snow,
healing our ugliness;
rising like the flowers
that garland the meadows;
breaking upon us like the ocean wave,
your love sweeps all away.

Handmaid of the Most High God,
servant of the King,
blessed bearer of the holy Child,
sing for us Magnificat—
our flesh exults,
immortalized by God.

Who Is This One Who Knows Our Pain?

Jesus heard that they had driven him out, and when he found him, he said, "Do you believe in the Son of Man?" He answered, "And who is he, sir? Tell me, so that I may believe in him." Jesus said to him, "You have seen him; and the one speaking with you is he." He said, "Lord, I believe," And he worshiped him.

John 9:35-38

Prophet, teacher long foretold,
light the darkness cannot hold—
who is this one who knows our pain,
love in whom we hope again?

THIS MAN IS FROM GOD.

Hurt like us, and healed,
what power does he wield
from our bondage to release
and to bring us to his peace?

THIS MAN IS FROM GOD.

We were blind, now we can see;
we were bound, now we are free.
Sin and sadness take their leave.
Who is he, that we may believe?

THIS MAN IS FROM GOD.

"You have seen him,
and he speaks to you now."

If We Follow You

As Jesus was walking along, he saw a man called
Matthew sitting at the tax booth; and he said to him,
"Follow me." And he got up and followed him.

Matthew 9:9

When Jesus recruits he doesn't give
    long speeches.
He found the tax office and said, "Follow me."
That was all. Not even a personnel form,
three letters of recommendation,
and place to put down "salary expected."
Matthew doesn't check about
    retirement benefits
or ask if apostles get Blue Cross.
Lord, you can't expect twentieth-century
    people to be so impulsive,
to trust in—well, nothing but God.
If we follow you we might have to feed
    the hungry,
give away the suit in the closet,
and stop pretending
that the prisoners and old people aren't there.

If we follow you we might have to give
    up grudges,
shake hands at the sign of peace,
break our cherished silences,
and even get along with our family.
Follow a teacher of love
and there's no telling where one will end:
on the side of mercy in a cruel world,

on the side of compassion, when we need
  tougher laws;
on the side of the peacemaker when we need
  bigger bombs.

A lot of other people say, "Follow me."
The crowd who set the fashions.
The boss. The rock idol. The boys who
  make it big.
The people who "play it safe," and "get ahead."
It's easier to be slaves and follow them.
It hurts to be free and follow you.

Come to the Banquet

For I am about to create new heavens and a new earth;
the former things shall not be remembered or come to
mind. But be glad and rejoice forever in what I am
creating; for I am about to create Jerusalem as a joy,
and its people as a delight. I will rejoice in Jerusalem,
and delight in my people; no more shall the sound of
weeping be heard in it, or the cry of distress.
Isaiah 65:17-19

Come to the feast.
I have made the earth a garden
of flowers and delights,
of rich foods and choice wines.
The grape is pressed,
the harvest gathered.
Call in the friend, the passerby.
Find the forgotten, the friendless.
Let there be no sorrow, no weeping.
Come in to my feast!

You with the weapon, put it down.
You with the clenched fist, open it.
There is a veil over your eyes.
I will remove it.
It has kept you from seeing
that you are all my children,
that I have desired you,
in all your variety,
to be the bride of my son.

Come, then, all you
begotten of my love.
My house is open,
the table spread.
The bridegroom waits.

Adapted from Isaiah

Inclusive

It's a motley crowd
whom Jesus makes his friends.
Sinners. Women. Pagans.
Tax collectors. Samaritans.
And even us.

Cana

Jesus the wine-maker,
sought-after guest!
Jesus the joy-giver
whose wine is the best!

A Strange Idea, God in Man

Just then a lawyer stood up to test Jesus. "Teacher," he said, "what must I do to inherit eternal life?" He said to him, "What is written in the law? What do you read there?" He answered, "You shall love the Lord your God with all your heart, and with all your soul, and with all your strength, and with all your mind; and your neighbor as yourself." And he said to him, "You have given the right answer; do this, and you will live."

But wanting to justify himself, he asked Jesus, "And who is my neighbor?" Jesus replied, "A man was going down from Jerusalem to Jericho, and fell into the hands of robbers, who stripped him, beat him, and went away, leaving him half dead. Now by chance a priest was going down that road; and when he saw him, he passed by on the other side. So likewise a Levite, when he came to the place and saw him, passed by on the other side. But a Samaritan while traveling came near him; and when he saw him, he was moved with pity. He went to him and bandaged his wounds, having poured oil and wine on them. Then he put him on his own animal, brought him to an inn, and took care of him. The next day he took out two denarii, gave them to the innkeeper, and said, 'Take care of him; and when I come back, I will repay you whatever more you spend.' Which of these three, do you think, was a neighbor to the man who fell into the hands of the robbers?" He said, "The one who showed him mercy." Jesus said to him, "Go and do likewise."

Luke 10:25-37

Teacher! What must I do to inherit
    everlasting life?
What armies do I need, what strife
to win the citadel, turn back to hell
the ancient foe?
There must be creeds to learn
and prayers to know.
I would have it all well organized,
thus and so.

At times, you speak so strangely
of an enemy within.
I thought the enemy was sin.
The sin of others.
Now you tell me they are brothers.
Sisters. All the world's a kin.
What applecarts you tip
with your astounding plan,
this awkward, strange idea
of God in man!

Who is my neighbor—you heard me ask,
and told a story! Then gave *me* the task
of speaking of *that man*.
The one who showed compassion.
"Go and do likewise." What could you mean?
Surely you know it's not our fashion
to copy foreigners and those unclean.

Go and do likewise! You could have said
to learn the Law
and warn that you would punish weakness—
every failure, every flaw.

But no. You praise Samaritans.
A man whose temple is not mine,
whose style of life and loving
you seem to think is fine.

I prefer the older way
of prayer and fasting
and warning to obey.
I must warn you, teacher,
there will be a ban
on radical ideas.
Like loving neighbor.
And finding God in man.

Someone Is Telling Us—Be Still!

Now as they went on their way, he entered a certain
village, where a woman named Martha welcomed him
into her home. She had a sister named Mary, who sat
at the Lord's feet and listened to what he was saying.
But Martha was distracted by her many tasks; so she
came to him and asked, "Lord, do you not care that
my sister has left me to do all the work by myself? Tell
her then to help me." But the Lord answered her,
"Martha, Martha, you are worried and distracted by
many things; there is need of only one thing. Mary
has chosen the better part, which will not be taken
away from her."

Luke 10:38-42

Martha is our patron,
no doubt about it.
We are anxious and upset about many things!

How will we pay the bills, survive,
have peace in our time,
a future for our children?
We are crowded, in a hurry
even on our way to play.
How can we sit around doing nothing
with so many problems to solve
and so little time?
God, you made our lives too short;
so much to do—the world's not right—
and what a waste of time
to make us sleep each night!

Martha, Martha,
slow down. Sit down.
And take up the Word of God.
That is, if you would like
to sit at Jesus' feet.
You'll find no instant recipes
for all your troubles.
The Word of God tells—stories!
About a man who kept on building
    bigger barns
but who was never satisfied.
His greed ran faster than his need.
Or the one who had a banquet every day
whose dogs ate better than the poor.

The Gospel has advice
like "Love your neighbor."
It's thoroughly impractical
except that hate has brought us
    down to death.
The Word of God makes promises, like
"Blessed are the peacemakers."
And tells us that the lilies of the fields
look better than we do
and we have the same Father
who is concerned for us.

The Word of God:
It won't pay the bills
but it might cut down on the things we buy
and make us less afraid to live. Or die.
Of course we have to feed the hungry!

Get ten thousand meals and greet the sun,
clothe the naked, heal the sick,
be Martha-Mary all in one.
But someone is telling us, be still—
to make a space in all our days,
slow down the race that's never won,
find time for listening, and praise.
Be like a child who does not fear.
Be still,
and know the Lord is here.

Hostess

Martha is the kind they describe
as "just a housewife."
Saints and sinners shared her dinners.
The man from Nazareth came quite often.

There's a Rumor in the Land

Now all the tax collectors and sinners were coming near to listen to him. And the Pharisees and the scribes were grumbling and saying, "This fellow welcomes sinners and eats with them."

So he told them this parable: "Which one of you, having a hundred sheep and losing one of them, does not leave the ninety-nine in the wilderness and go after the one that is lost until he finds it? When he has found it, he lays it on his shoulders and rejoices. And when he comes home, he calls together his friends and neighbors, saying to them, 'Rejoice with me, for I have found my sheep that was lost.' Just so, I tell you, there will be more joy in heaven over one sinner who repents than over ninety-nine righteous persons who need no repentance.

"Or what woman having ten silver coins, if she loses one of them, does not light a lamp, sweep the house, and search carefully until she finds it? When she has found it, she calls together her friends and neighbors, saying, 'Rejoice with me, for I have found the coin that I had lost.' Just so, I tell you, there is joy in the presence of the angels of God over one sinner who repents."

Then Jesus said, "There was a man who had two sons. The younger of them said to his father, 'Father, give me the share of the property that will belong to me.' So he divided his property between them. A few days later the younger son gathered all he had and traveled to a distant country, and there he squandered his property in dissolute living. When he had spent everything, a severe famine took place throughout that country, and he began to be in need. So he went and hired himself out to one of the citizens of that country, who sent him to his fields to feed the pigs. He would gladly have filled himself with the pods that the pigs were eating; and no one gave him anything. But when he came to himself he said, 'How many of my father's hired hands have bread enough and to spare, but here I am dying of hunger! I will get up and go to my father, and I will say to him, "Father, I have sinned against heaven and before you; I am no longer worthy to be called your son; treat me like one of your hired hands."' So he set off and went to his father. But while he was still far off, his father saw him and was filled with compassion; he ran and put his arms around him and kissed him. Then the son said to him, 'Father, I have sinned against heaven and before you; I am no longer worthy to be called your son.' But the father said to his slaves, 'Quickly, bring out a robe—the best one—and put it on him; put a ring on his finger and sandals on his feet. And get the fatted calf and kill it, and let us eat and celebrate; for this son of mine was dead and is alive again; he was lost and is found!' And they began to celebrate.

Luke 15:1-24

We run a Lost & Found department with
    our lives,
clutter them with forgotten people
and lost and wasted days.
Losing all those opportunities
to forget a quarrel and make a friend,
to call up someone, or just to say hello.
There's all the time we lost not loving,
sitting down to empty meals.
And the sleep we lost because of worry,
afraid to surrender to the arms of your care.

But there are days of finding, too:
finding health after an illness,
discovering how good it is
to eat, to walk, to live again.
And days that follow rain—
a world washed clean, inviting us to see
the trees and flowers, water, and the moon.
Some days we find some very precious things
like learning how to love again,
or that people hold us dear, and God is true.

In the end we all seem like losers,
born to hurt, to die.
We lose more than money,
more than autos in a parking lot.
We lose the way. And those who shared
the sweet moment of our being.
In the end we cannot hold, and letting go
we lose the day, and all that love
    has wrought.

There's a rumor in the land that there
    is more—
there's a story of a shepherd lifting up
    the stray;
and a woman holding tight
a coin that fell away;
a father searching through the night
and holding wide the door.
There's a rumor in the land, go tell the news,
ring out the sound, the sound of joy!
Rejoice with me, rejoice, for I have found
all that I have loved and feared to lose.

Upside Down

Jesus goes to sinners.
He even eats their dinners.
A radical? Indeed he is.
He turns losers into winners.

Wanted: Servants

A dispute also arose among them as to which one of them was to be regarded as the greatest. But he said to them, "The kings of the Gentiles lord it over them; and those in authority over them are called benefactors. But not so with you; rather the greatest among you must become like the youngest, and the leader like one who serves. For who is greater, the one who is at the table or the one who serves? Is it not the one at the table? But I am among you as one who serves.

Luke 22:24-27

We are here, Lord. Your good people.
We come to be comforted,
to pray for the poor
and hope they will become self-reliant.
The scriptures are a consolation to us
but lately it's awkward how often
the word "servant" occurs in the readings.
It seems out-of-date, a little quaint,
like days when the rich had butlers.
St. Paul insists "there is only one master
and we live and die as his servants."
And your Son, who could have become
        a scholar
well known in rabbinical circles,
says that he comes as a servant.
One of his stories implies
we should all be hirelings in his vineyard.
Does it mean we should serve the poor
        in person?

Can't we do it with our checks?
Will they be properly grateful,
and when we have borne the heat
    and burden
will there be some fitting recognition,
a citation, a reward?
God, you would make an unusual employer.
Your policies are generous—
too generous to some,
and too demanding to others.
We like your words of comfort
but only a fool, or someone in love
would work for you or your Son.

Day Is Done

(From the parable of the Master of the Vineyard hiring the workers, Matthew 20:1-16)

"Come into my vineyard
and I will pay you what is fair."
When we started, all the world was morning
and life itself seemed like each new day,
a thing unworn and full of promise.
It was enough to live.
Something left us. Was it gladness,
or our youth? Others passed, singing
a melody we too had known.

Day is done.
Go tell the owner
we won't argue over wages.
The light is failing
and we fear the night.

Where Are You, Lord?

Is not this the fast that I choose: to loose the bonds of injustice, to undo the thongs of the yoke, to let the oppressed go free, and to break every yoke? Is it not to share your bread with the hungry, and bring the homeless poor into your house; when you see the naked, to cover them, and not to hide yourself from your own kin? Then your light shall break forth like the dawn, and your healing shall spring up quickly; your vindicator shall go before you, the glory of the LORD *shall be your rear guard. Then you shall call, and the* LORD *will answer; you shall cry for help, and he will say, Here I am. If you remove the yoke from among you, the pointing of the finger, the speaking of evil, if you offer your food to the hungry and satisfy the needs of the afflicted, then your light shall rise in the darkness and your gloom be like the noonday.*

Isaiah 58:6-10

When the Son of Man comes in his glory, and all the angels with him, then he will sit on the throne of his glory. All the nations will be gathered before him, and he will separate people one from another as a shepherd separates the sheep from the goats, and he will put the sheep at his right hand and the goats at the left. Then the king will say to those at his right hand, "Come, you that are blessed by my Father, inherit the kingdom prepared for you from the foundation of the world; for I was hungry and you gave me food, I was thirsty and you gave me something to drink, I was a stranger and you welcomed me, I was

*naked and you gave me clothing, I was sick and you
took care of me, I was in prison and you visited me."
Then the righteous will answer him, "Lord, when was
it that we saw you hungry and gave you food, or
thirsty and gave you something to drink? And when
was it that we saw you a stranger and welcomed you,
or naked and gave you clothing? And when was it
that we saw you sick or in prison and visited you?"
And the king will answer them, "Truly I tell you, just
as you did it to one of the least of these who are
members of my family, you did it to me."*

Matthew 25:31-40

When did we see you hungry, Lord?
On the evening news as we finished dinner?
Was it all those children with distended bellies
and those who go blind from lack of
        Vitamin A?
And when were you cold and naked, Lord,
and we didn't clothe you, didn't care?
Was it last winter, when people froze to death
while their slumlords stayed in Miami
and the Christians were snug in their homes?
When have you been away from home, Lord,
and we didn't make you welcome?
Was it the visitor to the parish,
or the bewildered old man in the bus station,
or the daughter away at college,
or the refugees we see on television?

You can't mean Grandmother at the
        nursing center—
that's her home away from home!
When were you ill and in prison, Lord,
and we didn't visit you or fight for
        your release?
Was it Africa perhaps, or Iran,
or Chile, Russia, Korea, Palestine?
So many places.
Are you one of those political prisoners
their governments say don't exist?

We assure you, Lord, that as often as we
        find you,
we are willing to give what's left from
        the banquet
and all of last year's clothing
(as long as it's out of style).
But Jesus, you disguise yourself too well.
You look like just a man or woman—
not at all like your movies
or the pictures on our calendars.

Help us to see you, Lord,
before we are the goats of this story.

God of Mercies, Find Room for Us

These twelve Jesus sent out with the following instructions: "Go nowhere among the Gentiles, and enter no town of the Samaritans, but go rather to the lost sheep of the house of Israel. As you go, proclaim the good news, "The kingdom of heaven has come near." Cure the sick, raise the dead, cleanse the lepers, cast out demons. You received without payment; give without payment. Take no gold, or silver, or copper in your belts, no bag for your journey, or two tunics, or sandals, or a staff, for the laborers deserve their food."
Matthew 10:5-10

Lord, you too have called us
and sent us on a journey.
And if we are wise
we do not try to go it alone;
we need each other.
We need a little more equipment
than you allowed the Twelve!
But give us the same power
to confront evil and do good.

The apostle tells us
that "God chose us before the world began
to be holy and blameless in his sight."
When we are stained from the journey,
cleanse us,
and when we are wearied,
refresh us.

Only you know how long we shall travel,
but you have told us our destination:
it is our Father's house.
God of mercies, find room for us
at the table you spread,
at the banquet of life.

Galilean

The young rabbi has a way
of reversing things:
The humble are exalted,
the last wind up first,
and the dead are alive.

Lent

Nobody warns, "So many shopping days
    to Easter!"
No costly gifts, no monetary loss.
Easter seems too easy.
It is—if you forget the cross.

Good Friday

"Remember me,"
he said, and died.
The King enters heaven
with a courtier at his side.

Palm Sunday

Follow him!
(But not too close.)
Yell hosannah!
(Words are cheap.)
Crowds melt away.
And night returns.

The Savior rode an ass, the scripture says.
It must have taken quite awhile.
But the chariot, the warrior's horse,
just didn't fit his style.

We Don't Expect You to Answer Our Questions

As they were coming down the mountain, he ordered them to tell no one about what they had seen, until after the Son of Man had risen from the dead. So they kept the matter to themselves, questioning what this rising from the dead could mean.

Mark 9:9-10

Lord, we are your mortal people
and lately that means
we can't even pay the bills
for the ills our flesh is heir to.
Medical costs are going up again.
Babies are joys of the flesh
but they cost thousands to have
(and that's just the beginning).
We can't even afford to die
and doctors say they can't afford insurance
against the mistakes that might kill us!
Why did you think up dying anyway,
and is pain the only way to test us?

The pagans used to say
you were an angry God
who shot us down with fiery arrows.
And then that crowd called Israel
    said it isn't so!
In that story about Noah they say
you hang up your bow in the clouds.
St. Paul even shouts that you are for us!

(You got a good man for your message
when you knocked him down at Damascus).

We don't expect you to answer our questions.
You gave us a book full of answers.
Full of fairy tales and riddles,
        some would say—
but others call it Good News.
Perhaps we are missing the point
        (as is our custom):
In this case the medium *is* the message.
The Good News is Jesus Christ.

Like those friends of his on the mountain—
Peter, James, and John—
we keep on discussing
what it means to "rise from the dead."
The Holy Spirit might prompt us to discover
that life is worth it
and you are not a God of death.
I listen to the learned preacher tell me
that a new age has begun.
I hear it on the airwaves, too.
I know Jerusalem is called the Golden City
but the Jerusalem I read about
is a city of guns.

Still I believe, and want to believe still more
the apostle's words that
"We are God's handiwork,
created in Christ Jesus."
And "Christ is the power of God."

That power is the Spirit.
I have it— I can do more than
    keep the commandments.
And I have more to do than sit by rivers
    weeping over good times past.

I even believe that the temple Jesus cleansed
and promised to raise within three days
is the world I pollute
and the body I live in.
Let me get on with giving his Father worship.
It calls for good work and good life.
The eternal life that Jesus promises
is not just when I die—
it's when I start to live.
Eternal life keeps breaking in
with all those glad moments
when God is stronger than my doubt.

God is spirit. Be alive.

Moving Toward the Dawn

Magdalen was busy Easter morning
but in John's report
it isn't the news of the resurrection
that she brings, out of breath, to Peter
    and John.
Just a cry of bewilderment:
"They have taken away my Lord
and I do not know where they have
    laid him!"

As it happens to many of us,
the bottom had dropped out of her life.

Then we are told
how the disciples ran to find him
or at least find out what happened.
They don't sit around moping
at what might have been.
You can fill in the script from the scripture—
"There's the tomb; he's not here!"
No signs of struggle—the headband is
    folded up
(robbers don't do that)
and the winding cloth is still in place,
just as if, as if—
he "breathed" his way out of it!
All this is pretty exciting—
what do you make of it all?

What can anyone make of it all?
It's going to take more than detective work
to come up with the answer.

When we try to figure out Jesus' resurrection
the ballgame is too big for the park.

Then what hope is there?
Do we just read the scriptures and
        believe them—
"On the third day I will rise again?"
We are willing to read the scriptures
but it says, when Peter and John come to
        the tomb,
and referring to God's Word,
that even the apostles did not understand.

No, it doesn't.
It says as yet they did not understand.

There came a point when the light turned on.
Or rather,
when someone else turned on the light.
For St. Paul it was a flash of lightning.
For others, a slow dawning,
bits and pieces coming together,
like that time of confusion we all know
when one is neither dreaming nor waking
and reality swims together
into the moment called today.

It says, "The apostles learned to believe
        the scriptures."
They were Hebrew letters on a manuscript—
a scroll, a book of the prophets or psalms—
and they told stories about Israel
rising up on the third day,
or how the psalmist played his harp and sang,
"My heart exults, my very soul rejoices,
my body, too, will rest securely

for you will not allow the one you love
to see corruption;
you will open the path of life to me
and give me joy without end in
    your presence."

Suddenly they understood,
these Jewish followers of Jesus,
that Israel for them was a person
and he had been raised up;
he was God's beloved, his chosen one.
When the eyes of their eyes were opened
those ancient words were full of glory,
the very page seemed made of light.

It's as if some ancient race
had kept and treasured, all those centuries,
rolls of music, page after page of notation
that they could read but no one was able
    to play.
When the player came
and they discovered the secret,
then those black marks on paper
became a symphony more beautiful
than any music ever played.

The word the apostles came to believe
is that Jesus lives,
and what died on Good Friday
was death itself.

It is morning now,
and there is one great melody
for all the world to sing—
it is Easter, and we live.

You Delivered Him—Deliver Us

*So when they had come together, they asked him,
"Lord, is this the time when you will restore the
kingdom to Israel?" He replied, "It is not for you to
know the times or periods that the Father has set by
his own authority. But you will receive power when
the Holy Spirit has come upon you; and you will be
my witnesses in Jerusalem, in all Judea and Samaria,
and to the ends of the earth." When he had said this,
as they were watching, he was lifted up, and a cloud
took him out of their sight. While he was going and
they were gazing up toward heaven, suddenly two men
in white robes stood by them. They said, "Men of
Galilee, why do you stand looking up toward heaven?
This Jesus, who has been taken up from you into
heaven, will come in the same way as you saw him go
into heaven."*

Acts 1:6-11

O GOD WHO SENT YOUR SON
to walk the earth with feet that hurt,
who let him grow older
and swiftly hurl to death—
you delivered him.
Sin's great plot unplotted.
Darkness quite undone.
The chains brushed off
like some untidy threads
from shining garments.

YOU DELIVERED HIM.
No more sitting down,
weary from the journey.
No more the insistent cry
to sleep, to die.

WE ARE HIS JEALOUS BROTHERS, SISTERS.
And you have left us in our envy
with our watches and our shoes.
We are the people who keep time,
are held by time,
turn here to there
and today to yesterday.

DELIVER US,
as you did our handsome brother.
Deliver us
from clocks that make our children older
and airline voices calling out departures.

YOU ARE THE DIRECTOR OF THIS
SWEATY FILM.
Cut! We need a moment forever.
The one called joy.

Resurrection

Easter has a surprise
that many sermons never gave:
Those who die will rise
long before the grave.

Death is the tide.
It surges in upon the shore
and all our castles are no more.
But Christ is the rock.
And we endure.

Skeptics

Last on the cross, first at the tomb,
first to see the risen Lord—
the disciples do not take their word.
"This is women's talk!" they say.
A bias still around today.

Women Only

Mark and Matthew, John and Luke—
was it ordained, or just a fluke
that no woman wrote a gospel?
Men, as always, lead the way.
Except at the cross. And on Easter Day.

In That Faith I Live and Die

I know that my days
are poured out from the cup;
the time of my dissolution is at hand.
But he who gave me my beginning
is now at my ending;
I have no fear.

It is by his grace
that I am bold to say:
I have fought the good fight,
I have finished the race,
I have kept the faith.
And I believe that the Lord,
just judge that he is,
will award me the crown
of everlasting life.

In that faith I have lived;
in that faith I die,
and join all those
who have longed for his coming—
the Lord of glory
in whose love is my assurance,
in whose will is my peace.

Cf. 2 Timothy 4:6-8, 16-18

Ascension

Before your Big Departure, Lord,
would you record a message, let us know
the right decisions, ways to go?
Relax. You still can get the word.
The messenger—if we can hear it—
is called the Holy Spirit.

Give Us Your Holy Spirit

When the day of Pentecost had come, they were all together in one place. And suddenly from heaven there came a sound like the rush of a violent wind, and it filled the entire house where they were sitting. Divided tongues, as of fire, appeared among them, and a tongue rested on each of them. All of them were filled with the Holy Spirit and began to speak in other languages, as the Spirit gave them ability.

Now there were devout Jews from every nation under heaven living in Jerusalem. And at this sound the crowd gathered and was bewildered, because each one heard them speaking in the native language of each. Amazed and astonished, they asked, "Are not all these who are speaking Galileans? And how is it that we hear, each of us, in our own native language? Parthians, Medes, Elamites, and residents of Mesopotamia, Judea and Cappadocia, Pontus and Asia, Phrygia and Pamphylia, Egypt and the parts of Libya belonging to Cyrene, and visitors from Rome, both Jews and proselytes, Cretans and Arabs—in our own languages we hear them speaking about God's deeds of power." All were amazed and perplexed, saying to one another, "What does this mean?" But others sneered and said, "They are filled with new wine."
Acts 2:1-13

Like your disciples on Pentecost
we are gathered in one place.
It is called earth—small,
and a bit crowded,
but still room for us all.
It is the future that worries us.
We play rough games with each other,
and we are only a blue marble
in the game of the cosmos.
Indeed our only hope is that you hold us
in the palm of your hand.

We come from every nation under heaven,
in five beautiful colors and all kinds of
shades.
Some of us are new and sparkling,
others are a bit shopworn.
But who cares, if we can look to you,
for we have heard about your marvelous
deeds.
We see them in the stars and in our children.
From the Middle East to the Mississippi Delta
there is no place where we have not heard
about the marvelous things you have done.

Yet in our hearts we know
that we are still babel and confusion.
Give us a common tongue—
not of language, but of love.
Give us a common bond—
not of race, but of brother and sisterhood.
Give us—but you have already given us—
your Holy Spirit.
Then turn us back to life.

Pentecost

Father and Son
behold the work they have begun.
They breathe on our humanity
the gift of their divinity.
Come, Holy Spirit.
Make us one.

Trinity

Angels fear to go
where learned folk have trod.
Does the ant climb the mountain?
Does the creature study God?
Come, Holy Spirit.

Fire on Earth

Is there any way of bringing
fire to the earth?
Any way of guaranteeing
life after birth?
Yes. We've been told the secret
but we do not hear it.
It's called the Holy Spirit.
And the gift of God.

Late Bulletin

You know the message he sent to the people of Israel,
preaching peace by Jesus Christ—he is Lord of all.
That message spread throughout Judea, beginning in
Galilee after the baptism that John announced: how
God anointed Jesus of Nazareth with the Holy Spirit
and with power; how he went about doing good and
healing all who were oppressed by the devil, for God
was with him.

Acts 10:36-38

Tell us the good news, Peter—
it didn't make the late edition:
"The good news of peace
proclaimed through Jesus Christ
who is the Lord of all."
It's been reported in New Jersey
and points north, east, south, and west
that the man from Galilee
did not stop with his baptism
(ritual was not enough).
Power went out from him
and the world has never been the same.

Who was this "man for others"?
Peter doesn't give details!
"Beginning with his baptism
he went about doing good
and healing all those
in the grip of the devil."
We have some private devils
we'd like to shake off.

Is this power still around?
And when the darkness starts to fall
we need to hear that word again
about Jesus, Lord of all.
It's hard to believe him.
They haven't got this peaceful line
in Lebanon and Belfast,
in New Orleans and Palestine.
In conversations
and international relations
hostility's the thing.
Peter, tell it loud and clear;
the news we get from networks
isn't all that good!

He went through all the land
healing and helping
and that's how matters stood
when they killed him,
    the little evil men.
He died in the noonday
and darkness came again.
"And that's how it was,"
    Walter Cronkite would say
if he were covering Jesus that day.
Jesus isn't dead.
"God was with him," the apostle said.
That's how it was
with the man from Galilee.
What's the word in Georgia
and Duluth, Minnesota?
Is God with you and me?

Transfiguration

We know him well,
break bread with him,
know his kinfolk,
whence he came.
But on the mountain, in the light,
it was not the same.
Until he touched us.
Then we knew
we could walk with him again.

Transfiguration

Scholars still plod their weary way
to find what happened on that day.
Was the light on Tabor rising sun
that shone upon the Risen One?
Come, let us adore him.

Report from Tabor

Leave out nothing from the story!
What happened there? What did you see?
Nothing. Nothing.
We climbed a mountain with a friend
and for a moment, saw his glory.

Presence

Voices on a mountain
and visions are fine
but we do it more simply
with bread and wine.

Trinity

In the name of the Father,
Son, and Spirit.
That's the best we can do, God!
Have we come very near it?

We Gladly Come to Worship

*In the year King Uzziah died, I saw the Lord seated
on a high and lofty throne, with the train of his
garment filling the temple. Seraphim were stationed
above; each of them had six wings: with two they
veiled their faces, with two they veiled their feet, and
with two they hovered aloft. "Holy, holy, holy is the
Lord of hosts!" they cried one to the other. "All the
earth is filled with his glory!"
. . . Then I heard the voice of the Lord saying, "Whom
shall I send? Who will go for us?" "Here I am;" I said;
"send me!"*

Isaiah 6:1-3, 8

We gladly come to worship
in our comfortable and handsome church.
We're glad to know we are forgiven
and thrill to your prophet Isaiah
with his poetry.
We love his liturgical phrases,
"Holy, holy, holy Lord!"
But suddenly he sounds
like some recruiter, God's talent scout.
"Who will go for us?" he shouts.
"Whom shall I send?"

We got the message.
We can't say we weren't home when
    you called
or the letter got lost in the mail.
We are, so to speak, stuck with the hearing

and with one of two answers:
Yes or no. Stay or go.
But what did you, or Isaiah, have in mind?
To go to the ends of the earth?
Or to the parish hall, or the blood bank,
to the nursing home, or to still
    another meeting?
Is there any job description
of what the work would entail?
Is this what Jesus meant when he said,
"I was hungry and you fed me,
naked and you clothed me,
sick and in prison,
and you came to visit me?"

Who will go for us?
Whom will I send?
I am pondering my answer.
It's my nature to be cautious.
If it's a good day, Lord,
if the space is open on my calendar,
if the people are nice to work with,
I might give it a try.

We Are . . . Not Alone

*I take pleasure in three things, and they are beautiful
in the sight of God and of mortals: agreement among
brothers and sisters, friendship among neighbors, and
a wife and a husband who live in harmony.*

Sirach 25:1

It is impossible to live
unless we live together.
If at times we cannot stand each other
it is also true
that without each other we cannot stand.

Cain is still asking
the same angry question:
"Am I my brother's keeper?"
The answer is yes.
There is no one so strong who does not need
another person's strength.
Each of us falls by the way.
Each of us comes to the passion.

Time, like sand, runs through our fingers.
We are fellow travelers, pilgrims.
We ride the same subway, freeway,
hang from one bus strap,
    share the car pool,
and live on the same scared planet.

We are on the road to Emmaus,
doubtful, wounded.
But not alone.

Doubting Thomas

When you can't prove everything
and analysis is faulty,
the evidence contradictory
that supports the Easter story,
back off and wait. You might even pray.
Let God have his say.

Emmaus

Walk with a friend; share life together—
troubles, laughter, food, and drink.
Then share a wonderful surmise.
The Lord is closer than you think.

They Knew Him, the Stranger

*Now on that same day two of them were going to a
village called Emmaus, about seven miles from
Jerusalem, and talking with each other about all these
things that had happened. While they were talking
and discussing, Jesus himself came near and went with
them, but their eyes were kept from recognizing him.*

Luke 24:13-16

I've heard it said
that Jesus is not dead,
that others have found him
in the breaking of the bread.

They walked on a highway,
defeated, alone;
he became their companion
and lifted the stone.

He unfolded the story,
what the prophets had said;
they shared life together,
the cup and the bread.

They knew him, the stranger,
the man who was dead;
faith gave the answer
when love broke the bread.

I Ask Your Pardon

My God, you made me.
I am not dust of the earth
    that has no father or mother.
I am not like the beasts of the field
    that cannot love
and eat without giving you thanks.
My God, you made me, my body is
    your temple,
my flesh is the house of your Spirit.
And I come to you this night as your child.

I thank you for this day,
for whatever it has brought me
of food and delight, of new things and old,
of friendship and wisdom.
I thank you for this day which
    I shall never live again.
I have no regret at its passing,
for all life is your gift,
and whatever is good is not lost forever.

If I have misused this day,
or offended your other children,
my brothers and sisters in the human family,
I ask your pardon.
If I have brought grief instead of comfort,
if I have caused pain instead of easing it,
if quarrels or discord or deceit
instead of truthfulness have entered
    my speech,
I ask your pardon,
and I seek forgiveness with my heart.

And if others have hurt me,
help me to forget it.
Do not let me sleep with anger.
If I have not enjoyed your creation
as I should have enjoyed it,
I ask your pardon.
If greed has kept me from sharing
with my neighbor,
I ask for your help to be more generous.
O God of goodness and light!
I am a creature of earth,
and yet I am your child.
Forgive me my forgotten sins
and my offenses this day.
Help me to become the person
your love has created.
I praise you and bless you
for all the good things
which have happened to me.
And these I give back to you,
to share with me in eternal life.

O God, give me rest, and re-create my body.
Give me strength to enjoy your creation,
and to work for my daily bread
and others' needs.
Give me a good night.
Remember and bless those who have
loved me
and helped me,
my family and my friends.

I pray for all in trouble, all in pain,
    and all near death.
Be their comfort, and at the end bring
    us home.
O Thou eternal and all holy One,
O Thou radiant and beautiful One,
O Thou living and undying One,
O Thou powerful and gracious One,
    this is _____.
    I am going to sleep.
    Wake me to new life.
    I surrender to your love.

To the God Without a Name

And as for the dead being raised, have you not read
in the book of Moses, in the story about the bush, how
God said to him, "I am the God of Abraham, the God
of Isaac, and the God of Jacob"? He is God not of the
dead, but of the living; you are quite wrong."
                                            Mark 12:26-27

God of mountains and streams,
you refresh us,
you lift up our eyes beyond ourselves.

God of the skies and weather,
you shade us, warm us;
you turn the earth into a garden,
the fruit trees hanging low,
the bees wedding the flowers.

God of life and death,
you begin us, you hold us;
our names are written
on the palms of your hands.

God of music and all the arts
that make us more human,
you give us your vision;
you put your own eye into our hearts.

God of history,
of all the events that set us free,
you call us to freedom,
and to free our sisters and brothers.

God of Abraham, Isaac, Jacob,
God of people, love us.
Do not forsake us.
Call us your own.

Trinity

God is a circle, never a square.
God is a point that's everywhere.
God is one but God is three.
And God, I admit, is a mystery!

We Make You an Offering

I come to gather nations of every language; they shall
come and see my glory. I will set a sign among them . . .
to the distant coastlands that have never heard of my
fame, or seen my glory; and they shall proclaim my
glory among the nations.

Isaiah 66:18-19

We come from all those coastlands, Lord,
from Puerto Rico and Portland,
Delaware, and Duluth.
And we hope to see your glory.
We want more than the morning,
more than a sun that vanishes with night.
The glory of the leaves, dappled glory
that falls to earth and turns to ash,
not these nor apple trees in spring,
nor sons and daughters of our flesh—
they are not the glory that we seek.

We are the bold who dare to hope
for that sun which knows no setting,
for that life which knows no dying,
for that love which knows no parting.
O Jerusalem, God's holy mountain,
put our feet on your heights!

The Israelites bring their offering
in clean vessels
but we bring ourselves, and we are unclean.
Cleanse us, Lord.
We make you an offering
of our spent lives,
and our hope.

A Woman Clothed with the Sun

*A great sign appeared in the sky, a woman clothed
with the sun, with the moon under her feet, and on her
head a crown of twelve stars. She was with child and
wailed aloud in pain as she labored to give birth.
Then another sign appeared in the sky; it was a huge
dragon, with seven heads and ten horns, and on its
heads were seven diadems. Its tail swept away a third
of the stars in the sky and hurled them down to the
earth. Then the dragon stood before the woman about
to give birth, to devour her child when she gave birth.
She gave birth to a son—a male child, who is destined
to rule all the nations with an iron rod. Her child was
caught up to God and his throne. The woman herself
fled into the desert where she had a place prepared by
God., that there she might be taken care of for twelve
hundred and sixty days.*

Revelation 12:1-6

Hail Mary—
once we learned those words
and it was simple then.
Full of grace and blessed,
beloved of God, of women, and of men.

Not so the prophet's flaming pen.
We lose him somewhere
as the virgin mounts on high
and scholars and poets vie
to praise and analyze and help us see
just where her glory lies.

Be simple—poets, scholars.
Do not lose her in the skies.
Did the woman clothed with the sun
ever have a child run
in with stubbed toe
and sudden woe such as only mothers heal?
Is the Queen of Heaven still
the mother of a four-year-old
who brings her butterflies for jewelry
and his own choice stones to make
    her crown?

Now they make a slipper of the moon.
But did she not have children underfoot,
this Miriam of Nazareth?
A son named Jesse—Jesus—
the same who lost them on a pilgrimage,
then talked, like all his peers,
of things his parents did not understand.
Oh, yes. Do not be upset.
The woman with the twelve-star crown
still asks her peasant husband to light
    the candles.
It is dark now. And we need the light
that these three kindle
in the house God pitched among us.
No regality can rob us of that earlier plan
by which our flesh caught fire
and God became a man.

The courts of heaven welcome
but no less, the open door
where ordinary folk sit down,
eat, drink, find room for more.
The woman and her son,

the working man who calls her wife—
they are so ordinary.
We need them still to say
that living holds a secret:
God is near.
Not in the sun, moon and stars, but here.
Working, loving, visiting a neighbor,
coming home to rest, to live,
going up to temples to celebrate and pray.

We'll come at last to die—
Joseph, Jesus, Miriam, you and I.
Then let them open temples in the sky,
the ancient ark the prophets speak about.
Let poets and their fancy fly!

But not too soon.
We still live in the dark
and need a mother more than Queen
to say it's going to be all right
        (the mother's line).
There's an iron rod that breaks our fear,
a shepherd of the nations
whose pastureland is God.

Jesus, Mary. The first and distant promise
that we are Adam, we are one.
So trumpets, sound, and banners, flow!
Our spirit leaps in God
who still exalts the lowly.
And when the last dark passage has begun
light up all the friendly stars
and like our mother, clothe us with the sun.

We Give You Thanks . . .

The songs or psalms of praise on the following pages seek to unite us with the heavenly choirs whom Isaiah saw and heard in his vision:

> *In the year King Uzziah died, I saw the Lord seated on a high and lofty throne, with the train of his garment filling the temple. Seraphim were stationed above; each of them had six wings: with two they veiled their faces, with two they veiled their feet, and with two they hovered aloft. "Holy, holy, holy is the Lord of hosts!" they cried one to the other. "All the earth is filled with his glory!".... Then I heard the voice of the Lord saying, "Whom shall I send? Who will go for us?" "Here I am;" I said; "send me!"*

All things speak of God, if we know how to see them, hear them. They point beyond themselves and ultimately to the transcendent—borrowing Augustine's phrase, to the Beauty of all things beautiful.

. . . for the Lord of the Harvest

For autumn and the leaves of death
we give you thanks, O Lord,
and seek to praise
that northern lands can be a glory,
and men at peace find rest
from empty fields and spilling barns.
We thank you for abundant days,
for all the richer life
your son has promised,
more than eye, taste,
and even autumn can provide.

And present things:
books, faces, friends' return,
the fire's dance, the shouts of play,
the scarlet maple and the distant hills.
Your gift is like a wine,
pressed down and running over,
good measure for October days!

We give you thanks for banquets and for bread,
but more, that you are he who saves
the very leaf that falls
and seeks communion with the earth.
And we are never dead,
although we sleep and winter will return.
Gather us, O Lord:
We are the children of your love.

Lord of the harvest,
God of the beautiful world,
We are your glory,
and we give you praise.

. . . for So Many Signs

O God, we give you thanks
for your creative power
that has given us so many signs
of your love and goodness,
and a sign in our own children
that love takes flesh and dwells among us.

Above all we give you thanks
for the one who bore the child,
Mary, mother of Jesus,
and for the Savior of the world
who was born that silent night.
Let poets, singers find new ways
to fill with gladness Advent days,
to proclaim so great a birth!
Give the trees of the forest each a voice,
let the heavens declare, the earth rejoice,
and sons and daughters of the earth
join the angels in your praise.

. . . for Stillness and the Snow

We give you thanks, O Lord,
for times and seasons
and now for winter nights
when stars shine coldly bright
and dust is turned to diamond underfoot.

For winter days
when trees are stronger than the icy death
and hold in blackened limbs
the promise of the resurrection.
For opposites be praised:
for heat and cold,
for stillness and the snow
that sculptures every house and tree
and falls like some great absolution
to heal the wounded earth.

We give you thanks for him
whose birth we celebrate in winter
so all may know, may wildly know,
that love is stronger than the coldest flesh
and mercy blankets all the land
more surely than the snow.
We give you thanks for him
who makes more than children joyful
and does not cheat our laughter in the end.

Joyous Lord,
beyond imagining but not beyond desire,
we give you glory and our song of praise.

. . . for the Hope of Forgiveness

Father, it is right to give you thanks
for enabling us to live with hope.

The name of our hope is Jesus Christ,
he who faced death, the death of the cross,
and refused to deny that you are his Father
or that we who often wear the face of evil
are still part of that humanity he came
    to redeem.

For the hope of forgiveness flowing from
    your love,
for the hope of living even as we die,
living by faith and finally in gladness,
we give you praise and sing the angel song.

. . . for All Living Things

We give you thanks, O Lord, for times
and seasons,
for wheat that grows through winter snow
and now for spring and April promise
that life has many colors
and stirs within the womb.

We give you thanks for greening fields
and warming sun,
for winds that move the rainful clouds,
for all the flowering land,
the budding tree,
and seeds that break the tomb.

The brook runs free, the clod is broken,
and hope is sudden, like the swallows' flight.
Our sleep is deep, O Lord, as vast as death,
and waits the quickening of your word.

We give you thanks for him
whose newest birth we celebrate in spring
so all may know that beauty is not counterfeit
and earth has yielded up her dead.

Lord of color, Lord of all living things,
we are your glory, and we give you praise.

... for This Glorious Day

O God of earth and sky and all that live,
not thanks alone we give
but make the universe a song of praise
for this most excellent of days
when Jesus Christ is risen, Lord on high,
inviting us to live, and bidding death to die.

We too have pain and sorrow known
but know at last his story: We are not alone.
In that dark passage he has gone before,
unbarred the gate, flung wide the door
to life, to life! And love's embrace.

Upon this glorious day the night shall
        not descend,
nor shadows end the light of glory on
        his face.
Jesus, savior, friend, and kin
who wore our flesh and bore our sin—
he lives! The angels sing. Creation gives
a shout of Alleluia: God be praised
for Jesus Christ, and Easter days!

. . . for the Power Within

Loving God, we give you thanks
that you have called us to live and to love,
to be part of your creation,
to do your work and will.

We thank you for the power within us
that moves us to pray, to choose good,
    not evil,
the power which is spirit, the Holy Spirit
whom Jesus promised to give us.

It is the word, not the wind, that moves us,
and a voice within.
The fire of love is kindled in our hearts.

Creator Spirit, font of our own creativity,
source of all that is good and beautiful,
Spirit of joy, in whom Jesus rejoiced,
Spirit of truth, who helps us to understand
all that Jesus taught,
Spirit of wisdom and of fortitude,
in whom we stand firm in our believing,

we give you thanks that we are temples
    where you dwell
and lift our hands and voices to the
    eternal realm
where angels sing your glory.

... for the Love That Sustains Us

Creator of the world, lover and
    parent beloved,
Mother and Father to us, we give you thanks
that you have not left us without your name!
You sent prophets to proclaim the Word,
teachers to explain it,
believers to live it, and give it flesh once again.

You made us children of the light; you have
    not kept from us
the secret of the universe and our being:
You are more than wisdom and power.
You are the love that sustains all things,
that willed our existence and made us
    your people,
love that surrounds us and will not let us go.

That Jesus bore this love to earth
gives us great joy, for he is the one
who calls us friend and still breaks bread
    with us.
We live because you have shared your
    loving power
with those who made us and shaped us in
    your image.
O God of Israel, God of Jesus, God of the
    human family,
we join the stars and angels in your praise!

. . . for All Good Things

O Father, we thank you for all good things,
for the earth which feeds and delights us,
the place where we live, walk, play,
    and dance.

Praise be your name, O God,
for rain and sun, for day and night,
for life and the hope of tomorrow.

In our journey you have given us for
    our companion,
the One who abides,
who is Alpha and Omega,
our beginning and our end.

He comes to us in word and spirit
and in the community of faith and love;
through him we offer worship
and with the angels sing your praise.

. . . for All Your Carnival of Living Things

We give you thanks, O Lord,
for summer days,
for waterfalls and waves
that beat on lazy shores,
for the fruit of April's blossom
and gardens of delight.

We give you thanks for murmuring sound
and brilliant wing,
for all your carnival of living things,
birds, butterflies, and honeybees,
that cannot keep the secret of your art
but wears it in magnolia trees
and dandelions and green carpets
on the valleys.

We thank you now for laughter and for rest,
for animals and fish and time to play,
for friends, and love's embrace.
And for the hope that endless summer
is a hint of our eternal joys.

Lord of our happiness and sorrow's end,
we give you laughter, and our praise.

. . . for Your Most Radiant Gift

Father, we thank you,
we praise you,
for your most radiant and splendid Son
whose warm, bright love floods all the earth,
breaks every seed,
and brings us all to life.

We share the long and lovely days
when light is even more your precious gift,
remembering him
whose light has shone upon us all,
who like the August moon
marks out a path
across the dark waters of our journey,
and bids us walk, run, skip, and even dance.

Lord of the light and joyous giver,
we sing to you, and give our praise.

. . . That You Have Spoken

WE GIVE YOU THANKS
for all created things,
for your Spirit that moved
and made of chaos our universe,
that bid the waters yield dry land
and earth to bring forth life.

WE GIVE YOU THANKS
that you have spoken and we live,
that you are present and we are not alone,
that you love us and we should be unafraid.

MORE THAN THANKS
we would make the world a song of gladness
because you have given us Jesus your Son!
We are his body,
sons and daughters of the earth,
brothers, sisters, of the Christ.

HEAR US AS WE PRAISE YOU,
Father of us all.

. . . for Your Unseen Choirs

We give you thanks
for the earth you fashioned
and gave us for our home.

And for the power to speak and love,
to live as your children.

All creation is your Word
and Jesus your Word come among us.

We would make our lives an offering
and our voices a symphony of praise.

Let the heavens declare, the earth rejoice!
We are not dismayed that all things pass,
for your Word and those who hear it
are part of you forever.

And we join the unseen choirs,
the angels who proclaim your glory.

. . . for the Gift of Healing

O God of all holiness,
I ask the gift of healing,
the healing of my body
if that is your will for me
and the healing of my spirit
so I may live in peace.

There is no night or day,
no time of sleeping or waking,
when you are not present.
O God, your love begot me,
gave me life and faith
and all good things.
For these I give you thanks
and put myself wholly
in your loving care.

. . . for Us

Father, we give you thanks
that you made us, from the dust of stars
and the breath of your own being.
You have spoken, and we live;
you are with us, and we are not alone;
you love us, and we should be unafraid.

We raise a joyous cry because you
have given us Jesus, your son,
who shared our life so fully
he knew its dying,
and now bids us share his rising,
the new creation that he brings.

Through him we praise you
and join the angels in their song.

. . . for the Table We Set

We give you thanks, Lord,
that you have called us to live,
given us bread to eat
and wine to gladden our hearts.

The earth itself
has become a sign of life and a place
   of wonder,
our homeland, and the place your
   kingdom comes.

The table we set could be empty
but you have filled the whole world
with your abundance,
you who call all things into being.

We give you thanks for all
who gather in friendship and love,
who break bread and pass a cup,
but most of all for he who did this as
   our brother,
Jesus, who shared our pain and joy.

Through him we praise you,
and with the blessed in heaven
we sing to your glory.

. . . for the Word of a Friend

WE GIVE YOU THANKS, LORD,
for your gift of love,
the love which many waters cannot extinguish,
not even the torrents of death.

FOR THE LIFE THAT LOVE HAS KINDLED
and the more abundant life that opens
every day
with the beauty of earth,
the wonder of the heavens,
and the word of a friend.

WE GIVE YOU THANKS
for love incarnate in Jesus
who became our friend,
whose life is stronger
than all the powers of evil,
that life which is your last
and greatest gift to us.

PARENT OF ALL THE LIVING,
and lover of what you have made,
hear us, as we join the angels in your praise.

. . . for the Breaking of the Bread

Father, we thank you
first for life,
for creating each of us
and making us persons
through those who love us.
We thank you still more
for your son Jesus Christ
who gives meaning and hope to our lives.

And we are bold enough to ask for more,
that you give us Jesus this day
under the signs of bread that is broken
and a cup that is shared,
so that in our hearts we may know
we do not live for ourselves alone
and we, too, will find him
in the breaking of the bread:
in loving and serving each other,
and in the brokenness of life,
when we are healed.

We praise you, Father of us all.

. . . for Every Day

We give you thanks, Lord,
that you have sent Jesus among us
and he became the reason for our hope.

You have called us to be children of the light,
no longer to walk in darkness,
not even to fear the night of death.

You call us to live by your commandment
of love,
to recognize our neighbor as part of ourselves,
to see all things and all people
as part of your creation
and the earth itself as the home of
your children.

For this we give thanks and pledge our
faithful love
as we join the angels in their song.

... and Join Our Voices in Praise

We give you thanks, Lord,
that you have written a law into our hearts
and have given us a covenant
sealed with the blood of Jesus.
He did not leave us orphaned
but sent the Spirit, as he promised—
the Spirit that enables us
to choose good, not evil,
to keep the law that binds us
to one another, and to you.

O Maker of the heavens
and all that lives and has being,
the moon and stars praise you,
the trees of the forest praise you,
the waves of the ocean praise you,
the ninefold choir of angels praise you,
and we join our voices to their song.

. . . for This Beautiful Earth

O God, who has given us the beautiful earth,
not the sterile moon, to be our home,

You have made possible the oceans
that bathe the shore,
the fields that yield their grain,
the gardens that feed and delight us.

For all that lives is your gift of life,
all that grows is part of your creation,
and all that delights us
in the rainbow and the rose
is part of your eternal beauty.

For these gifts and more—
for life, and faith,
for each other, and for Jesus Christ,
we give you thanks,
and join the angels in their song.

. . . with St. Francis

Glory be to thee, my God,[1]
for the gift of your creation,
and especially for our brother, the sun,
who gives us the day,
and by whom you give us light.
He is beautiful, and radiant,
and of great glory,
and bears witness to you,
O most High.

Glory be to thee, my God,
for our brother the wind and the air,
serene or in clouds and all weathers,
by which you sustain all creatures.

Glory be to thee, my God,
for our sister water,
who is very useful and humble,
and precious and pure.

Glory be to thee, my God,
for our brother fire,
by whom you illumine the night.
He is beautiful, and joyful,
and strong, and full of power.

Glory be to thee, my God,
for the gift of your creation!

We who are part of your new creation
now give you thanks and praise.

[1]*from the Canticle of Creation*